By Rose & Frank Winn

The Adventures of Rose Bud

Let's be friends

Illustrated by usillustrations.com

2023

A wonderful story! This is the second book of three. The Adventures of Rose Bud, born with a rose over her heart and her quest to find her missing dad, is filled with adventure, hope, and the power of friendship. Rose Bud's determination to find her dad takes her on many exciting adventures. She discovers that the rose over her heart is not only beautiful but is very special. Rose Bud's message to everyone is, "Let's be friends."

@2023 Rose Winn & Frank Winn

ISBN 979-8-218-25128-4

All rights reserved.

Dedicated to my mother and Rose's Nana. A woman who had many special gifts and will always be our biggest fan.

It was a beautiful sunny day as Rose Bud paddled her leaf boat up the Laughalot River. The tropical air filled with the sweet scent of flowers and the soothing sounds of chirping birds. Rose Bud's heart was filled with determination as she embarked on her quest to find her missing dad. She remembered her mother's story of that fateful winter day when he had ventured out to search for food and never returned. She knew she had to be brave and follow the river, hoping it would lead her to him.

Suddenly, the winds howled, and dark clouds loomed overhead, Rose Bud's heart raced with fear. The once calm Laughalot River transformed into a turbulent force, its waters thrashing and churning. Raindrops pounded against her little leaf boat. Rose Bud was caught in the middle of a terrible storm!

The wind began to calm, and the rain eased into a gentle drizzle.

"Are you all, right?" Asked the Alligator, who had swum up beside her.

"Yes, I'm fine. Just a little buzzed," Rose Bud said.

"You did quite a dance on that river," said the Alligator. "I'm surprised you didn't lose that rose you are wearing."

"I'm not wearing a rose," Rose Bud replied. "I was born with it over my heart and that is why they call me Rose Bud."

"Well, hi Rose Bud, my name is Chick."

Rose Bud explained to Chick what happened to her father and her determination to find him. Chick offered to help her and told Rose Bud that she could ride on his back.

Rose Bud smiled at Chick and said, "Let's be friends."

The two of them continued the journey up the Laughalot River, their friendship budding.

"Who goes there!?" chirped the chicken.
How dare you step foot on the island of Winnahaha!?"

"We are so sorry," Rose Bud said with a sigh.
"We are hungry, and we saw there is a beehive
dripping honey from that tall tree."

"Hungry?" The chicken chirped with a feisty
demeanor and bold attitude. "What is your name?
And who is that green monster with you?"

"My name is Rose Bud, and this is Chick.
What is your name?"

The little chicken cocked her neck back, and jokingly replied, "Sure... and my name is Alligator."

The three of them laughed and the little chicken confessed that her name was Sam.

Sam agreed to help Rose Bud get the beehive dripping with honey but warned her about a pesky frog.

"Rose Bud," Sam chirped. "There's a frog named Mr. Otis at the foot of the tree, and he is very mean. Worst of all, he loves to eat ladybugs. The only thing that Mr. Otis loves more than a good-tasting ladybug is his hat. Mr. Otis loves his hat."

"Hi, Mr. Otis. My name is Rose Bud. Would it be all right if I go past you and get some of that honey hanging from the tree?"

"It certainly would not!," croaked Mr. Otis. "And if you try, I will eat you."

Suddenly, a gust of wind blew Mr. Otis's hat up into the tree.

Rose Bud thought for a second and said, "Mr. Otis if I help you get your hat from the tree will you promise not to eat me?

Mr. Otis, taken back by Rose Bud's kind gesture, croaked twice and agreed.

Without hesitation, Rose Bud turned to Chick and yelled. "Whip it, Chick! Whip it!"

Chick sprang into action. With a swift movement, he extended his strong tail and whipped it back and forth, generating a powerful gust of wind. It not only knocked down Mr. Otis's hat but also knocked down the beehive rich with honey.

"I got your hat back Mr. Ottis," Rose Bud said, her voice filled with satisfaction. "Now remember your promise. You will not eat me!"

Rose Bud made clear to Sam and Mr. Otis her desire to continue her quest to find her dad.

Sam told Rose Bud and Chick about an island further up the river called Sacasumoco.

"It might be a good place to search for your dad," Sam said. "Just be careful because it could be dangerous and there may be some enemies of a ladybug."

Mr. Otis agreed and said "I know the island.
It is covered with a lot of little slimy green creatures... yum, yum, croak!"

Rose Bud and Chick thanked Sam and Mr. Otis and waved goodbye. The two of them continued their journey toward Sacasumoco Island.

Rose Bud and Chick landed on Sacasumoco Island. The island seemed haunted and filled with mystery. "This island is giving me the creeps," said Rose Bud. "I'm not so sure this was a good idea."

"Don't worry, it will be all right," Chick said with broken confidence. Just stay close to me and I'll watch your wings if you'll watch my tail."

KIAI! (Attacking move)

Anatahadare! (Who are you)

"Say what now?!," Rose Bud shrieked.

"Don't look at me. I only speak alligator!" cried Chick.

"I am an Assassin bug and I want to know what you are doing here?"

"My name is Rose Bud, and this is Chick," gesturing towards her loyal companion. "We are looking for my dad."

"I don't care who you are looking for!" retorted the Assassin Bug. "I will chop you up, cut off that rose, and eat you!"

"Stop!" Chick protested. "You're not going to chop anyone, and you will not eat my friend Rose Bud. You don't even have a sword."

The Assassin Bug looked sad and confused; He told Rose Bud and Chick he had lost his sword in a battle with a panda bear.

Rose Bud paused for a moment. She asked the Assassin Bug, "If I get you a sword, will you promise not to karate chop Chick and not to eat me?"

The Assassin Bug hesitated but agreed.

Rose Bud looked around and spotted a Locus tree. She asked Chick to lift her up with his mighty tail while she reached out and grabbed a branch.

Rose Bud brushed off the leaves, carved a sword, and handed it to the Assassin Bug.

The Assassin Bug smiled. He lifted his sword in the air and all three of them cheered.

Rose Bud said to the Assassin Bug, "Let's be friends." The Assassin Bug agreed and bowed, "OSU… that's Japanese for yes and much appreciation."

Rose Bud and Chick said goodbye to the Assassin Bug and continued their adventure to find her dad.

Chick and Rose Bud walked until they came upon a pool of water, at the foot of a waterfall.

Chick asked Rose Bud, "How is it that you are able to make friends with everyone you meet?"

Rose Bud thought for a second, her gaze fixed on the rippling water. "I believe it has something to do with the rose over my heart," she said. "It reminds me to see the potential for friendship even in those who may initially seem like enemies."

Rose Bud and Chick smiled and gazed under the evening stars.

The next morning, Chick and Rose Bud continued their adventure up the Laughalot River.

They were not sure where they were going but were determined not to stop until they found Rose Bud's dad.

"Hey Chick," Rose Bud gasped. "This looks a lot rockier than the last time we were on the river and there's a huge rock right in the middle of our path."

"Don't worry," said Chick with a boost of confidence. "I can maneuver around it."

"Oh No, a monster!" screamed Rose Bud.

"Hold on Rose Bud!" Chick said in a panic. "That's not a monster. It's a hippopotamus!"

"Chiiiiick!," Rose Bud yelled.

Chick and the hippopotamus rocked and rolled until they both fell over the waterfall.

"Oh no," Rose Bud cried, as tears rolled down her eyes.

"What am I going to do now? I've lost my dad and Chick."

It started getting late. Rose Bud was lost and scared, so she began to walk swiftly through the jungle.

Suddenly, she came to an abrupt stop.
There was a very bad odor in the air.

Standing on a log was a peculiar-looking bug with a clip on its nose.

"Hello, my name is Rose Bud. Do you smell something funny?"

"No," snapped the bug. "I don't smell anything funny and why would ask such a mean question? I am a Stink Bug, and I will eat you."

"I'm sorry," Rose Bud said apologetically. "I didn't mean any harm. Please don't eat me and maybe I can help you."

"How can you help me?" asked the Stink Bug.

"You see." Rose Bud explained.

"I was born with a rose over my heart, and it has a very pretty smell. I will give you one of its pedals and you will not stink anymore."

The Stink Bug's eyes widened with curiosity and excitement.

Rose Bud plucked a petal from her rose and handed it to the Stink Bug.

Rose Bud took the Stink Bug's hand and said,
"Let's be friends."

The Stink bug and Rose Bud started to walk until suddenly Rose Bud slipped and fell into a deep dark hole.

Rose Bud was in the dark but she was not alone.

"Hello!" Rose Bud's voice echoed.

"Stink Bug?"

"Mom?"

"Dad?"

"Chick?"

"Is anybody there?"

"I can't see, I can't see... I'll see you in book 3!"

Rose Winn is a student at Full Sail University, where she is pursuing a degree in the Arts. She attended school in Fernandina Beach and Douglas Anderson School of Arts, where she began her journey. She has directed numerous productions in her community and is thrilled to add an Author to her list of talents. Working with her father Frank has been a blast and she hopes kids all over the world will enjoy "The Adventures of Rose Bud!"

Frank Winn was born in Yonkers, New York, one of six children. He is married to his wife Kathleen and their daughter is Rose Marie Winn. Frank is currently a resident of Fernandina Beach, Florida, and has spent 40 years working in Aerospace, Aviation, and Defense businesses. During this time, he worked as a Manager for the Space Shuttle Program. Frank invented "The Invisible Jump Rope" in 1992. He is currently working part-time as a business assessor and loves spending time writing children's books with his daughter Rose (aka Rose Bud).

www.ingramcontent.com/pod-product-compliance
Lightning Source LLC
LaVergne TN
LVHW070435080526
838201LV00132B/280